Figeater

Published by Gunpowder Press
Edited by David Starkey and Chryss Yost
PO Box 60035
Santa Barbara, CA 93160-0035

Front cover image: "Giant flower beetle, Mecynorrhina torquata."
Illustration by Richard Polydore Nodder. Handcolored copperplate
engraving from George Shaw and Frederick Nodder's *The Naturalist's
Miscellany* (1812).

ISBN-13: 978-1-957062-25-9
Library of Congress Control Number: 2025910174

www.gunpowderpress.com

Gunpowder Press is part of Gunpowder Poetry, a 501(c)(3) nonprofit
literary organization. The John Ridland Poetry Prize is supported in
part by the Santa Barbara Poetry Fund under the auspices of the Santa
Barbara Foundation.

FIGEATER

POEMS

ANDREA CARTER

GUNPOWDER PRESS • SANTA BARBARA
2025

Summer—Sister—Seraph!
Let us go with thee!

—Emily Dickinson

Contents

Platonic

I ordained
        the body once,
oracle, skeletal,
        an outline. Hung
skin, lost layer
        of muscle. How
to carry less
        weight when
the only way to
        ecstasy was
starve it.

My Bright Poison

Final Waste Burial, San Onofre Nuclear Power Plant, 2021

Only nothing comes
       from nothing, uranium
pellets hummed like bees

foraging the honey I love.

      I dreamed of smoke-less,
greaseless, ashless-ness,
        harmonies, clean energy

speaking perfect geometries,
devout as a Quaker's

clock, each gear, crank,
      and turbine automatic,
      theories, my steel core erotica.

      I believed, my hope, fusion—

      Then it all ended. The exterior taken
first, the physical containment. I couldn't

contain where my release seeped,
      my concrete buttresses, mirrors,
doors, and doorways, sinks and

      hoses, intake system
pumps, flow meters, my computers

installed backward. I did not
　　　　want to disown, transport
a sum of the whole. At night,

　　　　in the freight cars, my plunder
　　　　rattled the rails. I heard the song
ignite across the desert yaw.

The rod bundles, my secret kindling,
　　　　I corroded skin, light, and bone,

　　　　and the sea I sacrificed searches

for the cooling pools, the split
heat, for the smell of the burning.

The Power Company

I wasn't the girl you could take out to
        dinner or a movie. This was
        the movie. Off-white moon, gray milky

        blur, gnarled live oaks reached across
        the highway. Obsidian sheen on the Pacific. This
was as far as we would get. A bottle, a drive,

coming in for the close-up, and falling
        asleep before the credits rolled—
        I wanted your grip on my shoulder, your

        voice asking me to stay. I jumped barefoot out
        of your truck, pieces of us in my pockets,
December, the cold sand, fire pit smoke—this was

romance. Of course, there is no romance without
        pain. I zipped it all back into my jeans, feeling
        the way it worked down my legs, the tingling

        of it up my arms, numbing my fingertips
        as I put my hands up to stop the whirring
in my ears. I could run the entire city

on my electricity for as long as I lived—

Outside Atomic City

Is this where we get lost, face
        the great desolation, blinded
                      windows, a welcome sign?
The fissures are not done
        breaking—

        We had gone so far past American
                Falls, to get to the testing site,
      two nuclear fuel engines
                  hollowed deaf-making
                        machines, monuments of aborted
      transport, incinerate the thought—

                              Why
              scorch the skin, why unearth
                  the earth, why steal the empty
      from the empty mind?

Our atmosphere was burning. Just
                say what you mean, before
      the ground goes flying before
        our shock sustains the chain
reaction. Why stay? Because

                    the isotopes need more isotopes,
            but we follow the
    road, the terrible invention

                  of hope, and the sun still
      coming for us regardless—

Destination

For some time, all I thought I had done was flee,
        and what would that count for, a defeated army

unable to escape its armor, the clanking uphill drag
        and stumble? I lied, watched the right moment

pass with my eyes closed, packed and unpacked
        the car to estimate what would fit without arousing
suspicion—and the false starts, cutting the engine

        because the sound would say, I might just mean
it—but calculations create speed and lift and skin turns
        silver in proximity to sun. Ocean cities, the swimming

red and white houses, always, it's the ground that gets me—

Fear of Heights

"Every angel is terrifying."
—Rainer Maria Rilke

1. Will I be able to calculate the speed of falling as I am falling?

2. Three hundred and forty-nine Skytree stories left to go.

3. Does the velocity mean I won't see the tiny high rises, shrines, and track and field stadiums?

4. The sky wants nothing to do with me, so I hope grace will.

5. My fingers so numb from the security guard's sweaty grip as he tried to hold on.

6. The uselessness of my feet and hands.

7. How much I hate wind that shears to the bone.

8. Two young women in sandals laughing, standing on the glass portal taking pictures of their feet as if they were in midair.

9. The voices of those women fading like mites in my ears.

10. Could I please lose all sense of myself now?

11. Can I make myself lose all sense of myself now?

12. Do you see me, Tokyo, as I land, finally, not looking anything like an angel?

Seven Thousand Feet

We take elevation
      for what it is,
tiger lily, glacial

      sheer, a grave in the grass,
and we consider
         each gray idea coming.

      Tyler drove his head
         of cattle here, wrangled
through the field of boulders,

narrow crag openings. Scree
      slid out from under, year after
year scaling the mountains,

      and one summer he
         froze solid in the snow-
storm of 1882. Granite,

      manzanita, sandstone, and
bristle cone, such a kind of beauty
      can ruin you.

The Abandoning

She gripped the steering wheel
beside me in her car, parked in
the movie theater's empty lot. She

was going to leave him. The afternoon
sky of scrubbed aluminum reflected in
the melting ice puddles. Her blind

little white dog on her lap licked
its balding paws. The SUV ticked and
pinched as cold filled the interior,

our breath stunned the windshield
when we talked, her tears dripping like
welding beads. Semis rumbled on, full

of cut timber braced for the sawmill.
We met here on her way out of town,
out to the highway and the state

line to say goodbye, to be a witness.
I had watched her dead eyes, watched
her eat nothing, grow thinner until

I could almost see through her. The big
black suitcase loomed in the hatch behind
the back seat. I wanted to tell her anything

that would stop her from shaking, from
pulling herself apart. "I should stay. I
have to go." How dangerous is loneliness?

Leaving had seemed so easy, like cutting hair,
sweeping a floor, crossing the street. But
the winter wanted more. It was not him she

was leaving, but I did not know that
at the time. Later, I too would have my own
many lived lies. The rest of the gutted forest

tried to retain its balance, a yellow traffic light
blinked at the cross street, a cloud of gulls
flocked overhead and flew into the past.

Mirror, Mirror

Chase ghost train
hydraulics, the story
splits me into—

Snow White's
Scary Adventures—
grease, gas,
screaming acceleration—I am the child

who is crying—the wicked queen
opens her red lips—
bolts of blacklight—

the car brakes, pauses, scenes flap
back like bats—will I eat the gift
of apple poison, a pink
kind of evil?

I fear to be the maiden
who severs herself in half
for the transmigration

of parallel souls
on grooved tracks—

There is no safety chain
on this dark ride—
all the purity I do not
have piling up

on my frozen shell—and no
one to release
me from my glass coffin—

Days of Snow

piled up in me, I cross country skied

until the sun set. Headed for the
house in the valley below the pass. Started

a fire, turned on the space heater,
filled the coffee pot with water from the
bathroom sink

because the pipes in the kitchen froze
four months out of the year.

Inside my cheeks burned. I'd write about the
woods, the dense looming ahead

—it was a cold, uncomfortable life, but

I loved these moments by myself,

watched the wild turkeys fly, waved
to the solitary horse in the
meadow terrified for its loneliness
until the horse was joined by a donkey, and I felt
relief—

The big barn on the right caved its roof

after it had carried all that snow

without reinforcement, collapsed, its mouth
completely missing its upper jaw. It remained

like that well into summer, the summer my boyfriend and I had to leave the farmhouse, after he left a fire burning overnight.

I think he was seeing someone else, there were rumors about this—

The house was deemed unfit to live in, and we were unfit to live with each other, and I left

my body full of snow.

That Kind of Joy

It is so much harder to be still, to let
          in this urgent green, open to stone sky,
          fractal soil, tree-bark, and rain

          that came before, its mud slick
          ruckus—sometimes I feel like
I can take the bruise on my skin

easier than what my head will
          welt me with inside—Atlantic
          seal-back blue, I can stand

          the truth. Glacial lacerations
          mark the granite, here is where
the future starts—where the sun

first imagines a super-nova state, black-
          orange morning. The forest tells me what
          I need to hear—learn to love what is

          hardest to love—the boy on the bus
          this morning beat his head with his fists,
and cried when his mother made him stop—

I Can't Get Next to You

"I can make a ship sail, on dry land"
—*The Temptations*

As if a mind could know another
mind. Even when I stood bare

on the beach shivering, or when you
took off your shirt and threw it

into the street. We walked through
silver pistols of rain. I want to say

it was not us, but the place—so
much water flooded the intersections,

the security guards dogpaddled up
to the curb, alligators lurked in

alley pond seep. Our clothes twisted
together in the all-night laundromat.

The ruins floated like milk-soaked cake,
we found the rusted bicycles clinging

to the branches of trees, red and green
syrups from the shaved ice truck. You took

out your cellphone, photographed women
on the beach to take home. I watched

the other life you lived beside the one
with me. I smiled as hard as the cinder

block houses surrounding us. No, naked-
ness only seemed to make us worse.

Breaking Pelican Bone

        She tore apart
              the sunlit zones,
                    worn and moody,
            a hatchet shadow,
   before the attacks forced

   her structure free
           of skin. How does
               she witness, now,
        in her yellow
  eyesight, this end?

The water wields
      its aspic glassy-ness.
           Hermit crabs
   husk the rock pile
for empty shells,

        the sky is galvanized
            sheeting and salt lick
               clouds. I fear the snap
          echo, I fear her
      throat pocket
  cries full of sand.

Animal Mourning

We cried all night
when the old cat was dying in our bed.

We circled our bodies around him,
stroked his lion head, looked into his eyes blinded by seizures.

At the vet's we watched him
be put down,
but we could not bury him.

We took him home
in the cardboard box,
and put him in the freezer

on the right side
away from the ice cubes and stacked pizzas,

until we found a place.
later that spring, a hill
covered in salal and fern
overlooking the small lake
where no one would know—only us—

When you picked up those women
at the hotels near the freeway,
and slept with them, you were
solving the grief of so many things,

the cat, our marriage,
all the other addictions
requiring paraphernalia.

Did you weep over the cat with them
the way you did with me?

Did you show them the spot
where we buried the cat?

Did you dig him up and re-bury him again
with each girlfriend?

All that upheaval
of pine and soil and damp,
how we buried each other that year—

The Brutalist School

—William Pereira, architect, Geisel Library

Even a sign can be
        a sign—un-speak, un-
        write, un-translate—

        blueprints are also stories,
        not brutal but simple. Concrete
            looms a eucalyptus forest,

            platelet leaves swarm
        an almost blue-like
        sun, octagonal head

        full of eyes. All the words
        can do is smear their silent
mouths against thick glass—

The Stealing

All lava paths ran past
our window. I wanted us
                              to climb
the volcano, see the inner life,
the magma chamber. The guide
told us the path up was too
dangerous.
                  But I didn't know
you were my danger, that birth-
mark in your eye.
                        You said you
could tell the couple we
sat with at dinner were having
an affair, but how would you
know? I found it
                        exciting.
After this I would understand
you were having many women
but not
              this woman. We saw
the couple again, held back
by police at the airport for taking
tiny spiral seashells.
                              The woman
emptied gallon Ziplock bag after bag,
making white volcanoes on the plastic
customs tables. The shells splayed,
penitents on their knees
                                    meeting
the pyroclastic flow. We had no
right to spectate, to think we
were any better at doing
what we were doing.

What the Tulip Market of 1637 Could Bear

What profusion was I before?
In the brack of sand and mulch, farm
compost, rising above the North Sea, far

from the sultan, mathematical
form, a color to ignite Eden in the
hard gray flatness. Peel to my quick,

smuggled to Utrecht, gloved under
ground, more expectant
than midwinter sun. Later, I figure in still-

life paintings with flowers that could not
possibly bud at the same time.
All my manipulations bred without scent,

regrafted, seeded, stored
in burlap, in a cellar drawer, ragged
edge, the mania, assure the populace

to make it through another generation.
Beauty is trade, what you get for it. What is
value? Behead my bloom.

Once

The man I loved walked into winter,
and I followed—high altitude blue

and frozen white drifts, smooth
and round—we entered the glass

museum. My orange heart glowed
liquid for him, wrestling the steel

blow rod while the glass globe became
a cavern, a planet, an earth melting and

cooling—I could not imagine being
without him. I wanted to chase meteors

for him, swallow atomic bombs—
I could not keep him safe, but I did

not know I was not supposed to—
dusk there turned yellow, green,

tender, before the light disappeared,
Venus and all her facets piercing the sky.

The Other Abandoning

Better to capture it on film, the woman
who is driving is me. There

is my passenger, a woman who I don't want
       to let out my secrets to—rocks will hit
       the windshield, the yellow summer

will start to burn at the edges like
an old film, and the car will stop moving

as the road dives into the clouds—
       I stop the car in her driveway,
       her fixer upper house, the koi gone

from their frozen pond, mulch rotting
outside the car windows. What I

didn't want to tell her flies out
of my mouth—an old osprey, orange-
       puckered eye, webbed gray feet, over-
       plumage matted. I will not be able

to swallow the bird back down. I will
say I can't leave him, the man I have to
       leave, and she says she will do whatever
       I want. We cry because we will never

be the friends we are right now. I see
her years later, and she will tell me
it is too hard for anyone to really know
her, even I do not know her, even

after I felt I could trust her with all
of that overexposed film, sad documentary

      of my life. Everything flickers away
      in her art house that is empty now—

there are no summers or clouds
or roads, only silent films no one watches.

Acreage of the Missing

The farm on the other side
of the creek had a stand selling
pints and quarts—

       smelled their sighs in green plastic
       baskets of sweet grief,
       halved the vowels and

              placed them in the fold
              of our tongues. Wild
              fruit blood, fertility,

                     and April cruel except for berries—

                     But now there are no strawberries,
                     no sweetheart meat

             wrapped in seed shells. There are
             the clones, the giants the size of
             apricots, red with no

       taste of red, or the half-white one,
       greenish fur on its underside.
       The current pushed

south, flooding crop rows, clearing
up for a whiter, gray sky and milky
rain. This has come

instead of sun
and we fall off our maps
into sacrament—

What I Left on the Rural Routes

We ate the bleeding plums
right in the middle of the sun.
         I don't know what slept
         in my empty skull, Sacramento

         flood plain run. We cycled across
         the train tracks, swam until dark
in the deserted public pool,
chlorine ghosts stuck to our

skin. Her arms, my arms, flying under
the wings of the trees. Why did I
         fall apart that summer, lose all my
         muscle, land in the back of a squad

         car, a danger to myself. My wordless
         mind, a cloudless copper oxide
sky. I left her in the farmland,
her tears as hard as seeds.

When Horses Race Fire

Ripped lilac from the inside
out—wind, smoke—
roads blocked off,

hot December, they went
back to rage, back to fire,

the racehorses' story, track
times, the other side. (I mean
rain, I mean training, I

mean the art of cleansing)
pain, domestic, the first

association—the violence eats
roof, stalls, and stable. Come
burning and betting to be

finished—for speed, weight,
and flight, quarter seconds

to be shaved off, smell hair
and bone and handfuls
of fight. Un-face or de-face,

a ritual, prehistoric, out of pure
expanse, stars in the gut of night—

The gold, gold, grasses,
the blades, the four hundred
bodies of breath, fear, desire, they

could not stop the momentum,
to save and be saved, to
be what the light shows

us, those faces, and also
to be whatever enflames—

Interstate

I am a moving violation;
I am making the escape. Tar

and gravel, asphalt by
the mouthful, I meet the country

of new stars. Oiled axle muscle
on a steep grade, the flyspecked

windshield cracks. I am
the gasoline residue, fire

roads, forgotten forest
communes, cinder cones, and

dotted white line passages.
I can always go. But what

I want is to go back
there. But I am a sonnet

to hubcaps. I am a wish.
I am gathering speed.

I am the accident as it is
happening. I am the impact, and

the head injury, and the highway.

In Need of Tools

Affix a sound,
    sun, morning,
woodpecker knocks its
    beak back and

    forth. Sugar pine,
cedar, fir, carry
    hard altitude light—

We can solve
    an inch, straighten
    an edge, haul

hammers, mitre boxes,
    band saws. We trace lines,
meet corners, apply
    alignment theory—

Draw drywall ceiling hoist,
    Fit socket wrenches,
    stand ladders, beat nails—

Unhouse bats,
    bees, root veins,
cut, plane, frame—

Let's stop and plant
    our hands so deep,
we mountain ourselves.

Under This World

—Craters of the Moon, National Monument

I did not know we would begin to see ourselves
    so clearly, here,
      together. I wanted
our shared story, our cave theory,

crawling the lava tubes. We were underground,
    the sun behind us washed our silhouettes boneless,

      gray parabolas, shapes, not faces, not real arms or legs.
      I remember the cold, what exploded,
the caldera, the great eight-hundred foot
    rift—the distance between the body and

      the skin, the cold glassy rock, my
hand on the surface of not touching.
    There was a beginning to the beginning, crystal black
minerals, matter almost too simple. Holding your hand but not

      holding anything, really, only hanging
on—the painful
    knowing, what we would do to each other. I have
been the field of your punishment. Still

the light incises us, the real and the shadow, to know
    which is which, to find the idea
of love is not the act of love, who

would care for that discovery? How do
    we exist now that we are above ground?

Wild Thing

—Bolsa Chica State Beach

Conjure bird bone fragments,
into the salt, into the fresh,
new estuary, and the overcast

watches for survival. Bandit-face
terns have come back, ground
nest the pebble sand, plunge

feed, their white bodies dagger
the swells. Three oil rigs drill
down the deep offshore. Water

levels grow steep and infinite. Rise
from rust and exhaust, grafted
wetland flesh, ingress, urgent.

Origin Disorder

I will never know what caused
that rift, but I know
                       it swam
in my body like the massive
school of shiny Pacific anchovies,
splitting and
                      reconnecting,
dissociation, two new selves, in the green
outer swells,
                asking and answering
the same question, who am I when I am
remembering who I am?
                    Even
the neutrino, the smallest particle
of reality, interferes
                        with itself,
can change from muon to electron
and back to muon again. At some
point a stingray shadow sped
across the great groove
                      separating
the left and right mindfuls. All
I could hear were fledgling
swallows, their voices
                brighter than
the sun. I went
         blind just listening.

To Bury a Mother

There was nothing of her to bury
when she died, except the dust

I shook on the cliff, the mad Pacific
waited. More than a year later, she

is all water. See her from the lifeguard
tower, north of Seal's Rock. Blow spray,

humpback, she is coming to me. Now,
the dust gilds her new face, a crown

or halo of escaped bubbles but hard
crustacea, barnacles, tiny, stacked shell

cities of the feather-armed, the one-
legged, the immutable. Her flesh

textured asphalt, bituminous. Grooved
gullet up to the eye slit, barely open,

and baleen wide, she cries. I do not
want the mourning of us anymore.

I give her my smell, my infancy, the sound
of not being alone out there in the deep

blue of our history. I give her what I can,
I give her something like family.

An Ocean Feeding

Crab traps empty
the catch into pots,

shells click, fat
pouches pop, and

woodfire of tongue
light. No one will know

the hunger of us. Night
turns its sun-burned

back. Hunks of sea-
weed mix smoke. You

and I eat our own fill.
Heavy these bodies,

the sweet meat so warm,
and the water so cold.

Of Death and Sugar

      cube, crystal, hunt
for honey, treat me.
      Disappointment is—
all wars are the same.
      I never lost the taste,
      my mother purged
herself, but I refuse
      to starve with that athletic
effort. My tongue
      is ready. Glucose levels
too low, but the Fates are my
      ingredients. The nurse calls
to ask me if
      I am still alive—

Fish Knives

—after an exhibit at the National Ornamental Metal Museum

After fish pics and axes?
Forged finery,

with waves and thrashing
cartilage tails. I would

like to mine meat from fat,
my thoughts
                            separated
threads, brain stew still
marbling,

                    to cut and clear
off the bone back except
which is worth more? Use

of the knife spelled over-
fishing, mad rushes on

a thickness of
                            scales escaping
cargo boat wakes, great

awakening baptisms, mad
factory effulgent. Such taste

hastened cod, mackerel, even
the tender eel
                 undulated
out to waterways clogged

up in panic. Rich and gelatinous,
filling baskets, but for only

so long. The knife inspired a sense
of plenty until
                 the knife was

starving too. What is want? I
only want more.

Unrequited

Rough work, desire, what
      it all means to mean. I see your
         eyes everywhere. Moon

        shroud over this wide
           mouth of the valley. River, shiny
              tongue splitting rock. Stoplight,

              highway, sunflower. Your story,
          feather-weight boxer, amateur class,
      parting lettuce leaves in that farmhouse

        kitchen. Your concentrated
     art of knives. Tomato blood.
I am still hungry. Where you are food.

The Blue Heart

—after Elizabeth Bishop

See the blue heart of glass?
Coppery sheened surface,

as if the sea itself burned,
and then what shot through

was the black bone frame
work behind the sky over

outlined corrugated folds
of shimmering delta, and veins

of narrow county roads.
Farmhouses kneel at the wet-

land verge. We start with
a crack we have to fill, a head-

ache, homesickness. The fissure
that came as part of the design.

Then there was an end. Summer,
swimming pools, fire hazards,

in the enclosure that night,
I botched the affair, opened

the awaiting wound. I could not
love you the way you wanted,

and my anger made a white-
hot want that twisted, pinched,

and cut us off completely.
Later, I noticed scratches

at the sides, a network of tiny
intersecting lines, a chloroplast

pattern or icy epidermis,
a way glass might explain

the concept of touch. It is
a drop of water in its own drop

of water, the blue heart holding
inside each half, yellow

alfalfa butterfly storms.
Forgiveness is a work of art.

Ecotone

Egrets fold their plots and subplots, their
        figure-eight white necks, and stand in water
where stars glint, marsh gloss, another universe,
                planets stolen, keep metals un-mined—when
I was eight I thought I could fly if I fell

far enough from the sky, a way out of myself,
           or else it was out to the garage, smell of hammers,
the vise, the two-by-fours with red-stain cut
        marks—girls can leave the earth by
fissure, by pain of salt—or maybe bioluminate the night—

Deep Space Flyby

Jupiter has rings too—ammonia-
gas clouds and no real surface
to land on—like my dad and
his destructive hydrogen mass, fear,
anger, manic depression, years
of long silences—then he stopped
that afternoon outside the house, not
his regular custody visit, and needed
to speak to me. I looked more like
an adult even at ten, and my body

belonged to my stepfather. Everyone
knew, but I didn't know they knew.
And my dad knew. He showed up
out of the blue, handed me the manila
envelope, smoked his cigarette to ash.
I pulled out the photos, sound of silk.
"No one," he said, "has seen these, except
the scientists. Those are for you to keep.
Don't give them to anyone." Space

expanding in my hands—orange
striations, almost white grout, and
the Giant Red Spot, cycloptic eye, a gas

storm, hundreds of years old, a constant

hurricane, grasping, expanding,

feeling for a purchase, stability,

a place to collapse, fall apart, re-

accumulate—I thought he gave

me Jupiter because I could keep

secrets. I thought this was his way of saying

he loved me. But my mind was still so new,

still taking shape—what if, instead, he

gave me Jupiter because he wanted me

to love him, my Great Red Storm, raging

to be loved—

Stingrays

Colorless as the water where they prey,
their venom lives long after myth.
This is one way our love can decay,
colorless as the water where we prey.
Odysseus' son speared Odysseus that way.
A rich sting to rule beyond my death,
colorless as the water where I prey,
if venom is all I leave to spell our myth.

ICU Scene with Medusa

      She wakes up in a hospital bed
after the deep-down
      five days in a coma. This white
jellyfish, a floating backless

      gown, plastic-tubes streaming
tentacles, she runs, her bare feet
      slapping the florescent
lit hallway. The nurses chase her,

      their squeaking tennis shoes all
over. She held the catheter, and
      the nurses held the zip ties
to keep her still. Is this vanishing

a kind of crime? She didn't
      believe anyone would
believe her. What is poison? An opaque
      viscous? All is blurry, nothing

      is clear enough, not even instinct.
No one believes her
      story, but someone is always
using her head as a weapon.

Velellas on T-Street Beach

So many tar-tear drops—hydrozoa,
not like the moon jellies we knew,
those crystal threaded tentacles of sting

that might pinch or leave red marks
across the summer skin.
These were not jellyfish, said the experts,
the teenage boys growing their hair

longer, not ready to dodge the draft before
the Vietnam War was just another show
on TV. My fourth-grade teacher told us we

would not say the Pledge of Allegiance
because we were too young to know
what we were pledging—she was strident
and young, and I was completely in love
with her—the Velellas spread forth, a hundred
eyes, the bright green and yellow center

of their bodies like irises, and tiny translucent
amphitheater sails, eyelids to protect these
boneless oracles. The boys said the creatures were
man of war, we should be frightened, scream

our heads off. But the Velellas
were lost and unarmed, like the boys
and men and refugees we did not dream
were coming to us from the sea—

Homesickness

A violet whisper, bone
and feather batting air
so fast, his name flies

into the unknown. Home
to me meant not to
bathe again, the lie

that I had lied
about with him—

I wore my zipped-up
down-jacket even when
Santa Ana winds welted

one hundred degrees—
he would break down
the shower door anyway.

Now there's my ache,

the pyre he built in the garage,
and the nails and screws.

There is no mirror, no
dark, no birds crash into

glass, orange thoraxes
and white-tipped wings—
my blood still has no

color. I clean everything.

Flesh

I shut my mind to it—

Better to smell the orange
blossoms trapped
in the trees. The other boys

who had ugly things done
to them came
and had to show me—

Those oranges that still had
taste left in them, the pockets of
pith, what left a wax
on the lips,

I was too scared to ripen and then
too late with wasps
swarming in—

I couldn't wait

to get out of this town,
all the spit from the boys
wet on my back—

Fire Safety I

I cannot kneel before you,
summer of skin cancer. I open
      my veins, after I open my legs

      to the sun. The German shepherds
chase us through the chicken wire fences.
The six thousand feet of

forest, piles of needles, flying beetles
      awaits. Cabins clap together, roofs
      chap and loosen. It is too hard

      to live here. The road falls off
      the mountain, sunflowers and lupine
star. The safety inspectors require

whacking all the weeds to stumps.
Stray sticks and rocks nick foreheads
      and necks. We make this place less
      provocative, less whorish for a fire to

      want to touch, torch the ground all the way
      to bedrock. But the dust sparks, and
only the wild knows what to save.

Fire Safety II

Do not tease fire. Pull
    hand over hand, words

like leather gloves, rake
    up pine needles or pay

a thousand dollar fine to
    the county. Bark disgorges

fire easier than you can
    yell a warning. Blue smoke

rose yesterday, the haunches
    of a ghost ridge. Season

powers down the slope, slashes
    dry the pines, cedars, the brave

apple groves, hemlocks, lilacs, Joshua
    trees, even the Mormon

rock. Sun tempers skins of the sky. I
    change the rake's grip to my right hand. Scrape

the dead ground down to what is
    alive. A needle goes right through

the glove into my thumb. How
    the dead invade the living. I was so

sure I could pick up the mass all
        at once without thinking. Pull, pile, and

pack plastic bags for the dump,
        for the county, for my friend

whose radiation burns, rakes
        pain across her left breast.

Prevention is a hurting thing.

Rainfall

Mist fog, not real rain—
I drive to the library,

wind swells shop awnings,
chairs and tables lay on their

backs, ride toward the pier.
The world is lighter than the rain.

I float out of the car past flooding
gutters, blurred storefront signs,

the dark coming overhead reflects
me standing at the glass doors.

This town I grew up in, left,
have come back to again. I enter

and children crowd me to pass. What
are they reading? I return the book

of poetry the other poet told me
to read. Her poems drowned

the lights of a town in the distance
at night where she did not want to

return. I did not want to return
here, but I think I am supposed to

be here, walk this beach where
I learned to swim, where whales nudge

my sleep, migrating south,
making the ocean parental and

the rain keeping everyone
here safe, inside, together, now—

Reading a Mystery

A plan to escape detection,
I have been walked all over,
a tell-tale heart-break. Look

again in the mirror
I cannot tell if I am inside
a mouth, a cave, myself?

I counted all the characters,
spotted the murderer.
I thought for sure

I solved it, even the raven knows
the crime, placates the chaos, tempts me.
The gardeners push their wheelbarrows

full of red bricks from the fallen down buildings.
The men stop moving, become monuments, I watch
their wrinkles grow vines and leaves,

a sun surfaces,
the gods come down
plant a knife in the hand,

a lily in the throat. What is the meaning
of this story, the red herring you can tell
afterwards, the disguise, the past

history? Let the word write me.

Dusk Ode

Start the incantations,
salt bush, needlegrass, the Latin
names for the forty species

of yucca. I touch syllable

outflows of sand. Ghost
crabs burrow the tide flats,

pelicans flee their wings. Will I
find the trail back up the cliffs?
The black helicopters search for

what the water has not done
yet. Cassiopeia shifts her

chair, her head tied to

the star behind me. I listen
how the ocean takes back
all its mass, its fingers digging

the tender underneath. How dare
I compare beauty to beauty?

To Pose

—after Artemisia Gentileschi

What is self-portrait?
As if the self is the same

at every hour in every gaze.
Why pay for a model
and gold brocade? Use her
own flesh, neck, body, angle

her right cheek. Contrast
against royal peacock ink,

or bathe her adventure in
velvet pomegranate. How

could she fulfill the court
appointment of England if
she could not be her own

subject? Palette knife her silks
a color of crushed krill. There
is no self, no real or unreal, only
each moment, glazed, emerging.

My Mother Remembers Her Painting in Her Dementia

She wanted to paint orange
                skies above thick
black squares filled with pale
        blue. Paper remembers, folds, unfolds,

ramparts and turrets, one
                  thousand
migrating cranes spreading isosceles
in her head. A right

                  triangle connects
a spaceship dilemma with sea urchin twists.

        She required tiring detail: lipsticks, rouge, contour,
highlight, cake eye liner.

                 Desire and distress
make starfruit spikes open the spring center
of a heart stent.
             Now, the sun is running out

of red, and she is
        a nightmare of fire.

Queen of the Night

Epiphyllum oxypetalum

No need for the moon
if she is open after dark,

completely awake, a circus
of exposure. Fear to touch

her. She could slip her concentric
tongues around an index finger, or

the finger that used to wear
a ring for the pleasure of being

a de-flower, an already at an end.
Her blossom is a honeymoon, all

through the night and gone at the first
insistence of sun. Her dry sickle,

the pink cloak in the morning,
a real marriage with its hints of blood

and bloodlessness, a white-
on-white-on-white derangement,

spiked petals unlocking, un-fisting,
unleashing, her expulsion.

Throwing the Body

—and the doctor says it is not what she thought, you will
      need to be under surveillance for those swimming mad
         cells in your left arm, melanoma, deep. So, let right

      thumb touch index finger there at the vulnerable
       first knuckle. Hold the instrument that needs
         to leave your grasp, its tip piercing the outermost
        edge of your sight, but you don't look because

       you can trust this body,
         you can trust this muscle,
       you can trust this release,

       of ions, the stark arc of vision,
     javelin, stalled falling star. Mark
    the gold grass, mark the seven
   kinds of soil, mark the blood
of your honest right hand—

What Will Make Me Well

I stand in the line of bereavements,
behind the ones holding handfuls
of shells, buttons, teeth, feathers—

Even with the gates un-locked
the unvolunteered want to remain
single file, cannot face another face,
the same open mouth. Surgeons,

RNs, ambulance drivers wear
gurneys on their backs, pots and pans
bang outside like bats leaving their nests.

How blades speak to skull-bone, pluck
a fatty tumor from the amygdala.
All the voices here singing opera. Someone
went to the sun and came back

on fire. What else did I not know
of this red heaven interceding?

Sunbeamed

Burn, blister, cancer—
                    I admit it,
I love to eat radiance, make
my own white dwarf—

What they calculate
in the worlds of alternate
measurement, the ghost body.
                    Let two
centimeters be enough for
 a clean kill—

The light undid my cells. What
can I say? I don't look too
long, I do not try to understand
what is not mine to understand. I feed
fusion and solar flares—
                    I am a fuel for joy—

At the Edge of the Lost Coastline

Where my heart should be
      muscle is a pink jellyfish that gorges on
hurt with its unmeaningful stings,

      and you are in there. I misidentified
the queen. Please forgive me for being
         afraid. I wish I had known how to know

      how to love you. What is that
flower? Jasmine, of course. The five-armed
         petioles meet at the center of the center-
fold. Everywhere there are cliffs, and

         the strange sadness of strawberries,
leaves seize distilled green time, landfill is
      landslide down to the ocean. But you

      still set all the boats on fire. If I am
         struck again, let me be the fool, please, let
me open my mouth full of bees.

A Heatstroke

1. If I close my eyes, I will see the dry lightning scars behind the sunlight in Mexico City.

2. You and I watch the clouds gleam above the pyramids above the orange, gold, and mint green city houses, and so many empty water bottles.

3. We sit on the concrete edge of the garden's waterless fountain, and I dip my hand, feel for what is missing.

4. Please call the fire department to unspool those long hoses and spray my skin off.

5. How am I unable to sweat? What did the temperature turn me into?

6. My insides will tenderize me first in an acid bath of digestion.

7. I have a head full of thirst, but my throat is swollen.

8. I stare down the drain of the silver tiled shower looking for the giant lake under this city.

9. You help me fight my body fevers with handfuls of ice and call me back from the God of the Sun.

10. Damp white hand towels dry and crust across my body.

11. Can you unwrap me like a mummy to see if anything is there besides my shriveled black tongue?

12. Tell me to believe in the love between oxygen and hydrogen, whatever kind of love that is.

And There Was a Sun and It Burned Me

Here under my epidermis is
a paradise lost, and my cauterized
sleep is at war with the Office of Transla-
tional Languages. What is left to give
up? My charred flesh, black teeth, black tongue,
a final, Biblical, skinless body?
Anger writhes like moray eels and free
tail bats. I offer myself to the grief
angels who feed me molted feathers glint-
ing with chips of ice. Desire is
a spoonful of needles. My cold soul
is a mound of salt. My purgatorial
plasma glows beyond any black hole,
beyond any undiscovered second sun.

The Pewter Society

What is not even shiny or
rare, we pour

ourselves into the cast
together, hold whatever time there is

with each other, or
sometimes just hold each other—

I still don't understand tin mixing
copper and lead, ellipses,

a pi value, a kind of whole-
ness. Metal of the dailiness, undecorated,

the glorious-not-this, but pliable, durable,
not pure, not sacred, but

constant like gulls can lift
an ocean in their wings, or fire

burns under a Siberian perma-
frost all year long. Shape,

form, then melt down and
make new, imperfect silver suns, blue

moons to light the foggy fields.

The Welder

It is not the same story,
      the mother needs the man, and
      so, needs her daughter to be

a kind of Hephaestus,
an arc, electrode, spark. Watch
               those leads like snakes

rope around them.
The daughter is the work,
the conjoining joint, testament

between her mother and
the man her mother sends
          her daughter to

in order
to make him happy. These things
        happen. All the daughter needs

   is current. She holds
   steel together, she makes her
own lightning, she burns human eyes—

Coming Across a Rattlesnake

Black lattice weaving
                white pear ripeness,

I thought selflessness to be
                without a self, a deep

rootless socket, a skin
                with no flesh in it. What

ached inside still kept me
                awake, the spies turning over

my soft secrets to the outside.
                Hawks scythe the violet blue

and wait for me to make my
                one false move. I coil

the land of my skin—sandstone, quartz,
                and tourmaline. I made

my sex a camouflage. Discover me.

Fire Diary

—San Bernadino National Forest, 2020

Feed foothill flanks,
        sugar pine, white
bracted manzanita,
        click cinder

teeth, bite wilted pine
        needles. Fist fingers
sweat steering wheel,
        tight-throated children

parch in the back seat. Peel
        the highway skin. Baby
cramps in her mother's womb,
        blister and updraft,

churn cloak smoke,
        torment root
systems, fill red
        embolisms squeal,

        gold sap boils.
Where?
        Where else to go?

The Work of Summer

I race the sun
in the wild mustard field,
the monarchs lace

the northern hemisphere
of my lungs. Boredom
is dangerous, chambers

enclosed in sugar maple
rings, daylight opens each
night at its seam. Out

of the granite boulders,
scree, out of hiding from
my own body, out of

hiding from myself,
I am a honey, and a wax,
and a new gold light.

I run to the scent
of water, and my head
is a beehive.

Cassini, Molto Crescendo, 2017

"It will become a part of Saturn."
—Earl Maize, Program Manager, Cassini Spacecraft Mission

The gold is what transfixes,
both her aluminum midsection

and perpendicular magnetometer
wrapped in lame thermal cloth.

Cleopatra would have had no
chance. That's why you don't see

the three radio plasma wave
antennas at first, filament thin

and delicate, three daddy-long
legs sunbursting from her side. Her

crown, a high-grade antenna dish
which she will use as a shield

for the mission descent. Boudicca
braved no barrage like this. Still

her senses are her exponential
power. She is of the earth and

not of the earth—to see, feel,
touch—more human than human.

In her Orphic turn she faces us,
not because she is unsure, but

because we don't know what
we think we know, and she blinks

back those last images, icy rings,
Saturn's south pole, and becomes

her subject, Saturnian wonder
unseen, this final falling gleam.

My Spring Awakening

When I kissed that girl, we
said we were practicing to
do it with someone else. Now,

April smell, waking worlds,
hearts with seeds. The berries,
might taste like a sour future—

I feel the fruit redden my lips,
I eat my words. Language
is always the ripest body—

Blood Mother

Cactus fruit, blood pear—is it
the mother or the child who is
more difficult?

                      I wanted her
to be more than she could be.

I was a swelling throat in sickness
a hunger for
                  so much water.
She was my stigmata, central
nervous system, the thrust
that love madness sustains.
                      Was this love?

                    These straight pin
spines set up to thread
a murder's connections, photos
of the dead, gunshot residue,
circumstantial evidence—

Was I what she wanted to give
birth to? A monastery of seeds,
                  a mouth of tongues
whispering, when do we lay aside

our war pride, when do we give
up, call our truces, and sleep
inside each other's promises?

Seal Skin

Forty or so, slick, merging, they
equip the dock, make
caves for each other to

take cover, the Harbor Sheriff pod.
When I am too alone in my
aloneness, and my heart feels

like liquid, I come to see them.
When I hate the God that is or is
not, and I want all who I wanted who

never came close to me, I ask, return
me into this body of bodies,
land my flesh next to

next. Let their heaviness
lumber me, fat and fin, before
the herd heaves whole, submerges,

and where I lost my place on land,
I'm whatever space needed
filling in the subtidal zone.

Ode To the Red Tide

I lived my life to become
someone else,

my mother's idea of a bloom.
She hoped

I would not eat
but smile, perform
that one-handed

trick, what turned the boys
on or not.

My mother taught me
not to say anything, no one
cared what I thought,

thinking would hurt, confuse
the real. Use

distraction, like
cutting a woman in half—

Now, my ocean is full
of algae. Ochre gems

crowd the surface like
armor on fire, until the water
turns into women fighting—

Figeater

I am an Eve
            before Eve—

            metal-green
shell beetle, I gorge
the overripe peach
flesh inebriate—

            secondary
wings of my pink
climactic triptych
unfold what

I hold,
my own sweet
sun-beamed seed—

            I am all
the fruit I want—

ACKNOWLEDGEMENTS

Versions of these poems have appeared in:

Amsterdam Review: "Platonic" and "What the Tulip Market of 1637 Could Bear"

Anacapa Review: "The Work of Summer"

Catamaran: "Origin Disorder"

Clover: A Literary Rag: "Cassini, Molto Crescendo, 2017"

Comstock Review: "That Kind of Joy"

Crab Creek Review: "To Bury a Mother"

Dogwood: "The Brutalist School"

Fourteen Hills: "Interstate"

Painted Bride Quarterly: "Figeater"

Quartet: "The Abandoning"

San Diego Poetry Annual: "Once," "Rainfall" and "At the Edge of the Lost Coastline"

SWWIM: "Queen of the Night"

Terrain: "Breaking Pelican Bone" and "Fire Diary"

The Big Window Review: "Stingrays"

The Common Ground: "The Other Abandoning" and "The Pewter Society"

The Florida Review: "The Blue Heart"

Zone 3: "The Power Company"

I am grateful to Gunpowder Press, Chryss Yost, and David Starkey for their work in creating this collection.

Thank you to the Wednesday poetry workshop at San Diego Writer's Ink and Ron Salisbury. Thank you to the Bread Loaf Writers Conference and the Napa Valley Writer's Conference; special thanks to Tomás Q. Morín, Carl Phillips, Donna Spruijt-Metz, and Brenda Shaughnessy.

And love always to my friends and my family.

About the Poet

Andrea Carter is a poet and writer from Southern California. Her poems have appeared or are forthcoming in *Mississippi Review, Crab Creek Review, Amsterdam Review, Comstock Review, Terrain, SWWIM,* and *The Florida Review*. A finalist for the Bellingham Review Poetry Prize, she received the 2023 Steve Kowit Poetry Prize. She teaches at UC San Diego.

BARRY SPACKS POETRY PRIZE

Dear Empire, poems by Holly Karapetkova

Burial Fragments, poems by Keith Ekiss

In the Cathedral of My Undoing, poems by Kellam Ayres

Accidental Garden, poems by Catherine Esposito Prescott

Like All Light, poems by Todd Copeland

Curriculum, poems by Meghan Dunn

Drinking with O'Hara, poems by Glenn Freeman

The Ghosts of Lost Animals, poems by Michelle Bonczek Evory

Posthumous Noon, poems by Aaron Baker

Burning Down Disneyland, poems by Kurt Olsson

Instead of Sadness, poems by Catherine Abbey Hodges

DRYDEN-VREELAND BOOK PRIZE

Three-Day Weekend, poems by Christopher Blackman

ALTA CALIFORNIA CHAPBOOKS

Alba and Other Songs, poems by Fred Arroyo

The First Amelia, poems by Amelia Rodriguez

On Display, poems by Gabriel Ibarra

Sor Juana, poems by Florencia Milito

Levitations, poems by Nicholas Reiner

Grief Logic, poems by Crystal AC Salas

FULL CATALOG AT GUNPOWDERPRESS.COM

JOHN RIDLAND POETRY PRIZE

Figeater, poems by Andrea Carter
Sad Animal, poems by Joshua McKinney

ALSO FROM GUNPOWER PRESS

Learning to Drown, poems by SM Stubbs
Empty Me Full, poems by Catherine Abbey Hodges
Frangible Operas, poems by Susan Kelly-DeWitt
Before Traveling to Alabama, poems by David Case
Mother Lode, poems by Peg Quinn
Raft of Days, poems by Catherine Abbey Hodges
Unfinished City, poems by Nan Cohen
Original Face, poems by Jim Peterson
Shaping Water, poems by Barry Spacks
The Tarnation of Faust, poems by David Case
Mouth & Fruit, poems by Chryss Yost

CALIFORNIA POETS SERIES

In Praise of Late Wonder, poems by Lee Herrick
Downtime, poems by Gary Soto
Speech Crush, poems by Sandra McPherson
Our Music, poems by Dennis Schmitz
Gatherer's Alphabet, poems by Susan Kelly-DeWitt